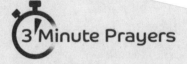

3 Minute Prayers

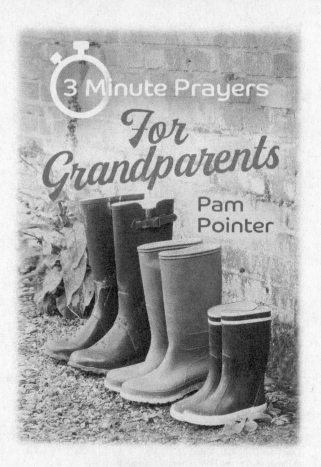

3 Minute Prayers

For Grandparents

Pam Pointer

kevin
mayhew

kevin mayhew

First published in Great Britain in 2019 by Kevin Mayhew Ltd
Buxhall, Stowmarket, Suffolk IP14 3BW
Tel: +44 (0) 1449 737978 Fax: +44 (0) 1449 737834
E-mail: info@kevinmayhew.com

www.kevinmayhew.com

9 8 7 6 5 4 3 2 1 0

ISBN 978 1 84867 985 6
Catalogue No. 1501606

Cover design by Rob Mortonson
© Image used under licence from Shutterstock Inc.
Typeset by Angela Selfe

Printed and bound in Great Britain

CONTENTS

SECTION 1

Anticipation

SECTION 2

Baby stuff

Children

Teens and beyond

ABOUT THE AUTHOR

Pam is a writer, speaker and photographer whose work reflects her observations of the natural world and its human inhabitants.

Why Didn't God Create Me With Green Hair? was Pam's first book, published in 1999. She has written a number of other books, plus many magazine articles on subjects as diverse as sleeping on the pavement in the Wimbledon queue, the work of hospital chaplains, and the merit of cows. She has contributed columns to local and national newspapers, broadcast morning thoughts for local radio, written an RE syllabus and teaching outlines, and writes meditations for an international magazine.

Pam is married with three daughters, three sons-in-law and five grandchildren. She enjoys being a homemaker, walking in the countryside, watching period drama on TV, blogging on her website: https://pampointer.wordpress.com/, and listening to 1960s rock music, Classic FM and Test Match Special. Pam is passionate about God, and Jesus is the solid rock on which her life is built.

INTRODUCTION

Nobody can prepare you adequately for being a parent. You muddle through, doing the best you can for your children, hoping and praying that they'll become happy and responsible adults. Now your children are grown up and you're going to be a grandparent! Are you prepared? It's been said that being a grandparent means having the fun without the responsibility. Is that true? In my experience, yes – though, because we're family across four generations, we all work together to support each other in good times and less good times. We share laughter and tears, joys and sorrows, ups and downs. We aim to share and care, following the example of God our Father and Jesus our brother and friend.

This book invites grandparents to pray for their grandchildren throughout their lives. Each daily piece invites you to read, pray and think for a few minutes as you bring the youngsters to Father God.

ANTICIPATION

WILL I BE A GRANDPARENT?

... the Father, from whom
every family in heaven and
on earth receives its true name.

Ephesians 3:14, 15

Well, here am I, Lord,
with a married daughter.
You know what's on my mind, don't you?
Will I be a grandparent?
Yes, I know,
it's not my shout.
It's their choice.

Some couples decide not to have children.
Would I find that easy to accept?
Probably not.
But help me to recognise
that whether it happens or not,
is not down to me!

Is the love I have for my daughter conditional?

Or do I love her unreservedly as God loves her?

HOW LONG?

This is the story of Jacob's family.

Genesis 37:2

Jacob's family was huge, Lord.
Twelve sons and umpteen grandchildren.
I'm finding it hard, Lord,
that all my friends
seem to have grandchildren
and I don't.
I suppose I exaggerate;
it's not true that they all have grandchildren;
it just seems that way.
And those who do
are full of how wonderful it is.

A few are a bit more sensitive
and pussy-foot around me
as if I'm tainted with something nasty.
They mean well.
I don't know which attitude is worse.
How much longer before it's my turn?
And Lord,
I know I must be very careful
not to put any pressure
on my adult children
to produce an infant.

How sensitive am I to the make-up of other
people's families?

I REMEMBER

**Jacob prayed, 'God of my
grandfather Abraham and God
of my father Isaac, hear me!'**

Genesis 32:9

I was slightly in awe of my grandparents, Lord.
They were a bit severe,
rather old school I suppose,
and I had to make sure
I behaved properly in their presence!
My grandpa said grace before meals – in Latin!
Benedictus Benedicat.
I hadn't a clue what it meant
and didn't dare ask.

My granny collected pigs,
china ones that were lined up in size order
on the mantelpiece.
Woe betide me if I touched them . . .
What will I be like as a grandparent,
if it happens?
Will I be indulgent,
or disapproving?
Will I know how to talk to a small person
after all this time?

How do other people see me?

Am I severe?

How would I come across to a small child?

THE AGE THING

Now that I am old and my hair is grey.

Psalm 71:18

Will my grandchildren think I'm old, Lord?
My grandparents always seemed ancient to me.
A bit like the cartoon image
of a white-permed-hair old lady
with glasses on the end of her nose,
and an old man with a walking stick.
You sometimes see that sort of image on
    road signs.
Well, that might apply to my own parents
who are still alive and kicking
but I'm a generation down from them
and still fairly sprightly.

I go to the gym,
play tennis, and can hit the ball really hard
as long as I don't have to sprint to it,
can certainly out-run toddlers,
if not teenagers,
and am generally pretty fit.
And, joy of joys,
when I told the hairdresser I'm nearly 70,
she said I didn't look a day over 60.
You're as old as you feel, they say,
and on a good day I could be 50
though some days I feel nearer 80.
Perhaps grandchildren will make me feel
    young again.

Some grandparents are 40, others are nearer 90!
Whatever their age, to their grandchildren
they'll seem old!

5

CONTACT

**Some people brought their babies to Jesus
for him to place his hands on them.**

Luke 18:15

O Lord,
you encouraged parents
to bring their children to you,
and you touched the little ones
and blessed them.
It must have thrilled their parents
to have their children affirmed by you.
How much contact will I have
with my grandchildren?
Will I see them often,
or not?

And what about physical contact?
What's appropriate
and what isn't?
I need to get it right.

Are you a hugging family or a handshake family?

Think about the different ways in which people
express affection.

MODERN LIFE

Noah had no faults and was
the only good man of his time.
He lived in fellowship with God.

Genesis 6:10

Lord,
if my grandchildren think I was around
   on the Ark,
will they think I'm completely out of touch
with the realities of twenty-first century life?
Does it matter if they think
I'm an old fuddy-duddy?
Will they ask me whether I knew Noah
or Isaiah?

Time won't mean much to them,
at least not in the first few years of their lives.
I expect I'll learn more from them
about today's technology
and culture
and trends
than I know already.
Sounds like it could be great fun.

Life has changed hugely since your childhood!

How well have you adapted?

MY CHILDREN

My father and mother may abandon me,
but the Lord will take care of me.

Psalm 27:10

Help me, Lord,
to love my own adult children
with the same sort of devotion
that you show to each human being.
I loved my children
before I knew anything of grandchildren.
Don't let me transfer my love
from my child
to my grandchild.
Love is one of those wonderful things

that isn't contained in a measured amount.
There's always enough love
to share with all the family.
So help me
to continue to love
and support
and affirm my own children
whatever the circumstances.

How much do you love your own children?

Do you tell them you love them?

8

ANCHOR IN THE STORMS

**We who have found safety with him are
greatly encouraged to hold firmly to the hope
placed before us. We have this hope as an
anchor for our lives. It is safe and sure . . .**

Hebrews 6:18, 19

I was never very close to my grandparents, Lord,
and certainly never saw them as an anchor
in times of trouble.
Maybe it was because they didn't live nearby
and communication then wasn't as easy as it is now;
no text messaging and no social media.
All families have wave-tossed times.

I'm always grateful
for the way my children support me
when I'm going through a tough period.
Help me to be an anchor for the family
when it's needed
and to be calm to comfort
as and when required,
remembering that you are the anchor
in my life.

How well do members of your family cooperate
with each other?

Could it be better?

BLEND

**Jacob took all his descendants with him:
his sons, his grandsons, his daughters,
and his granddaughters.**

Genesis 46:6, 7

Family relationships, Lord,
can be very complicated,
perhaps more so these days
than in previous generations.
Half-brothers,
step-sisters,
one-parent families . . .
You know how it is, Lord,
and it's not easy.

Help me to be an unbiased stalwart
in our family life,
to show kindness
and love
to each member of the family,
whatever the complications
of the relationships involved.
And if I can be a stabilising element,
then show me how to be so.

How can I be a stabiliser in my family?

MY CHILDHOOD

When I was a child, my speech, feelings
and thinking were all those of a child;
now that I have grown up, I have no
more use for childish ways.

1 Corinthians 13:11

I expect you remember
what I was like as a child, Lord.
Not always the perfect daughter,
or kindest sister.
I fell out with my brother
and scowled at my mum
to her face
and behind her back.

Help me not to expect my grandchildren to
   be perfect.
May I be a peacemaker
when necessary
and always be ready
with a listening ear.

Switch on your memory bank and recall your
own childhood or that of your children.

Think of the ups and downs and who acted
as peacemaker.

11

HOPES AND EXPECTATIONS

'I show my love to thousands of generations
of those who love me and obey my laws.'

Exodus 20:6

Well, all this so far, Lord,
has been hypothetical.
Thank you that, whatever my status,
whether I have grandchildren or not,
your love is constant
for me,
for my children,
for all children everywhere.

You gave your followers
a new commandment
to love one another
as you love us.
Maybe thinking about the possibility
of being a grandparent
will stand me in good stead
even if I never become one.
It may at least make me more understanding
of other grandparents
and of their grandchildren.
But to be honest,
I still hope it will happen to me!

Observe grandparents out with their
small grandchildren.
How do they engage with each other?

What evidence can you see of God's love
exemplified in the love between the generations?

BABY STUFF

OUCH

When her baby is born, she forgets her
suffering, because she is happy that a
baby has been born into the world.

John 16:21

Well, Lord, it's happening.
We got a phone call
to say our daughter is in labour.
Ooh, it brings it all back.
I remember quite clearly
that unnerving rush to the hospital
in the middle of the night
and then the breathing
and the pain

and the pushes
and the not pushes
and more breathing
and then the command,
'One last push!'
and the relief on the arrival of the infant.
And now we're playing the waiting game again.
I hope she doesn't take too long
for all our sakes!

Much of life is a waiting game.

How do you cope when you don't get the
instant results you might like in a situation?

THE PHONE CALL

Your daughter-in-law . . . has given you a grandson, who will bring new life to you.

Ruth 4:15

You know what my son-in-law said
on the phone?
'Hello Grandad!'
Oh, Lord,
how exciting is that!
It's happened.
I have a grandchild.
I want to shout it from the rooftops,
text all my friends and relations,
but I mustn't.

It's their news,
not mine,
so I must wait
and let them share their news.
But I can hardly contain myself,
I'm that thrilled.

Ponder the miracle of new life.

3

FIRST SIGHTING

May you live to see your grandchildren!

Psalm 128:6

Lord,
our son asked
whether we'd like to go and see the baby.
Would we ever, Lord!
They don't keep them in hospital very long
    these days.
I remember my mother saying
she was on bed rest
in a nursing home
for three weeks after she had me!
Nothing to do with mother or baby
    needing treatment.

It was just the done thing.
Now they shoot them out of hospital
a few hours after the birth.
Fear of infection I suppose.
Anyway, we went to their home
and met our grandchild.
He's so tiny!
Tiny toes,
button nose,
snuggled up in a shawl
and with a little cap on his head.
He opened his eyes
and we saw his tongue
poke out in a silent gesture of
'Where's my tea?'
He looked fine.
Our daughter-in-law looked weary
but beamed with delight.
A lovely new little family.

Recall the moment when your own child was born.

4

BABY CRIES

He was crying, and she felt sorry for him.

Exodus 2:6

Lord,
poor little Moses,
stuck in a basket
on the river.
No wonder he cried.
And was heard by a princess.
Well, this grandad
is learning again
about a baby's cries.
I'd forgotten how strong a baby's lungs are.
What a din!

How any parent interprets a baby's cry I
    don't know.
I found it tricky to fathom out
what my baby was trying to tell me.
Hungry?
Wet?
Tired?
Grumpy?
I imagine they're trying to fathom it out too.
I hope the new family
will be able to bond together
and work it all out
one day at a time
through the sleep deprivation
and bewilderment
that accompanies the arrival
of this all-consuming new person
into the family unit.

How can I reassure my child that it's normal for
a baby to cry?!

NAPPIES AND BOTTLES

Be like newborn babies, always thirsty . . .

1 Peter 2:2

Lord, will I be expected to change nappies?
Is it one of the privileges of being a
   grandparent?
Or one of the chores I offer to do to help out?
Can't say in all honesty
that it thrills me over much,
but I'm willing – I think.
And the bottle?
I think I could manage that all right.
Seem to recall that it's the temperature
   that's crucial.

You have to test it on your finger first
if I remember rightly.
And then there's the palaver of sterilising,
but I expect it'll all come back to me OK.
The practicalities can't have changed that much
in thirty years,
can they?

What do you see as your responsibilities for
your children and grandchildren now?

TODDLER TIMES

I walk in the presence of the Lord
in the world of the living.

Psalm 116:9

Lord,
our grandchild has gone through the sitting
    up stage,
then learnt to shuffle around
on bottom
then knees;
now he's stood up against the sofa
and is ready to take his first steps.
And metaphorically he's taking his first steps
towards independence too

though there's still a lot of time
before that becomes complete.
Actually,
does independence really ever completely happen?
I like to think that humans are interdependent
and that we all need each other.
Even when my youngsters flew the nest,
I was grateful that they still came back
from time to time,
still wanted to have contact,
and still saw us as family together,
even though they had their own family unit too.

How good were you at letting your child out on
a longer and longer lead until he was ready to
launch out on his own?

7

SUPPORT

**Our leaders gave their full
support to the people.**

Nehemiah 4:16

Long-distance relationships aren't easy, Lord,
and I regret
that one of our children
is a long way from the parental home.
I respect their situation
and want to do all I can
to be supportive across the miles
but Skype support isn't quite the same
as hands-on support.

Help us to remember
that there is still an invisible link
that keeps us together
despite the different locations.

How can links be kept over long distances?

ADVICE (OR NOT)

**I will give you good advice and share
my knowledge with you . . .
You have ignored all my advice and have
not been willing to let me correct you.**

Proverbs 1:23, 25

Help me, Lord,
to remember
that my children are grown up
and now they have their own family.
Help me to be willing
to give advice
when I'm asked,

but not to barge in
and interfere
by giving my opinion
when it's not asked for.
If I'm asked,
please give me wisdom
as I consider what is best
and help me to be sensible
and practical
and loving
in what I say
and how I say it.

How can I build a good relationship with my children, given their new family situation?

9

HANDS ON

**Whatever you do, work at it with all your
heart, as though you were working for
the Lord and not for human beings.**

Colossians 3:23

Now here's a tricky one, Lord.
My son and daughter-in-law
want me to be a hands-on grandpa.
They'd like me to do quite a lot
of childcare so they can both work.
I'm not sure whether this is
a step too far for me.
I still want to maintain a life of my own
and I'm not sure I'm patient enough

or fit enough
to look after my grandson
for even one day a week
let alone several.
Help! What should I do?

How do you get the balance right between
having your own life and helping out with
your grandchildren?

HANDS OFF

**Homes are built on the foundation
of wisdom and understanding.**

Proverbs 24:3

I'm not sure, Lord,
how to work this relationship
with my granddaughter.
Her parents are very keen
that I shouldn't do anything
that isn't in line with their wishes
and I agree.
I respect that they're her parents
and I wouldn't dream of
going against their wishes.

At the same time
it's hard not to be allowed
to have a bit more involvement.
Are her parents unsure of themselves?
Or do they think I'm incapable?
I know I'm not as sprightly as I once was
but I'm not totally decrepit.
Oh, for wisdom
and love
and understanding
all round.

What was your attitude to your parents when
you had a child of your own?

THE WONDER OF THE HUMAN FORM

**You created every part of me; you put
me together in my mother's womb.**

Psalm 139:13

Oh, Lord,
what a miracle!
I'm just overwhelmed
by the intricacies of the human form.
Only you could have thought up
such a complex way of putting life on earth.
From the ant
to the elephant
to the human being,

what mastery!
And when I look at my grandchild
and see how much she has developed
in the first months of her life,
I'm astonished at the progress.
Helpless at first,
now a running toddler
who's learning to jump
with both feet off the ground,
who's experimenting with speech
and discovering more and more
of the world around her.
Thank you for her brain,
her smile,
her sparkling eyes,
her mischief,
her curiosity,
her whole being.

Am I keeping myself as physically fit as possible,
so I can play with my grandchildren?

SECTION
3

CHILDREN

TIMES TABLES

The city ... had a great, high wall with twelve
gates and with twelve angels in charge of
the gates. On the gates were written the
names of the twelve tribes of the people of
Israel. There were three gates on each side:
three on the east, three on the south,
three on the north, and three on the west.

Revelation 21:11-13

Lord God,
you seem to like numbers
more than I do.
Is twelve your favourite number?
Or seven?

You are a God of order
and so you probably enjoy times tables.
I used to chant them at school
and we got a sticky star if we got them right
and a gold star if we could do all our tables
from two to twelve,
plus, would you believe,
fourteen and sixteen!
I'm re-learning my tables now
as my grandson is learning his for the first time.
He has all sorts of convoluted ways of
    doing numbers
which even his dad finds tricky to understand.
I want to take an interest
in all that my grandson does
and to enthuse,
even if numbers don't enthuse me
perhaps as much as they should.

Do you take sufficient interest in your grandchild's
work such that he wants to share his discoveries
with you?

THE ARTS

Praise him with trumpets.
Praise him with harps and lyres.
Praise him with drums and dancing.
Praise him with harps and flutes.
Praise him with cymbals.
Praise him with loud cymbals.
Praise the Lord, all living creatures!
Praise the Lord!

Psalm 150:3-6

I love music and the arts, Lord.
But was I a mean mum
when I wouldn't let my son
learn the drums?

Flute I could cope with,
trumpet I might have tolerated,
but drums and loud cymbals?
Did I deprive him?
It's fine once they have mastered the art,
but the learning can be excruciating
to the mother who has to supervise practice
in the early days.
Help me to encourage
my grandson rather more readily
than I encouraged my own son.

You might have a child prodigy for a grandson.
But you might not.

Either way, are you ready and willing to listen to
his efforts in the learning process?

3

SOWING AND HARVESTING

They sowed the fields and planted grapevines
and reaped an abundant harvest.

Psalm 107:37

Thank you, Lord, for the fun
of sowing seeds with my grandchildren.
They scatter the seeds liberally –
beetroot, carrot, flowers,
all over the place.
It's fun to grow beans
and raspberries and strawberries
and once I took them to a pick-your-own farm
and we came back laden!

The fun is in the doing
but also in the picking and eating
and a shared meal with my grandchildren
is a treat.

Think of the privilege of sharing your knowledge,
skill and enjoyment with little people.

4

NATURE'S BOUNTY

You make springs flow in the valleys,
and rivers run between the hills.
They provide water for the wild animals;
there the wild donkeys quench their thirst.
In the trees near by, the birds make
their nests and sing.

Psalm 104:10-12

Children are nearer the ground than me, Lord,
and they notice things with wonder
  and fascination.
A dandelion clock for me to blow,
a buttercup to hold under my chin,
a wriggly worm, a slithery snail.

Thank you that I can share the children's wonder
as I spend time with them.
Thank you that I have time to give to them,
to examine a leaf,
to crack open a horse-chestnut shell
and see the shiny conker inside,
to look for birds
and to listen to their song
and to hear my granddaughter
say with awe,
'Look, the peacock has put up his umbrella!'

How is my joy at the created world enhanced by
my grandchildren's joy?

ACTION STATIONS

Bad people will get what they deserve. Good people will be rewarded for their deeds.

Proverbs 14:14

In my day, Lord,
we played Cowboys and Indians.
Now it's Star Wars or Pirates.
Children learn about goodies and baddies
through playing.
I'm not sure that the goodies always win
but I guess that reflects real life.
At least in the end
we know that when you wind up history

evil will be defeated for ever
and justice and goodness will prevail.
Meanwhile, Lord,
I need to make sure I know the basics
of Star Wars
and Pirates
so that I can converse and play along
with my grandson.

Reflect on good and evil and think how
these aspects of life are in the lives of our
grandchildren and their playtimes.

READING

**Your word is a lamp to guide me
and a light for my path.**

Psalm 119:105

Lord,
my grandchild has learnt to read
and can now choose his own books
from the library in town
and from the school library.
May the books he reads
be uplifting and fun
and so enthuse him
that he'll also want to read your book, the Bible.

Help me to show him how it's the best book ever
and is there to lighten his journey through life
and guide him in your ways.

Are there ways in which you can encourage a
love for the Bible in your grandchildren?

7

SHOW AND TELL

**Grandparents are proud of
their grandchildren . . .**

Proverbs 17:6a

I'm chuffed to bits, Lord;
my grandson has come to visit
and has brought some things
to show and tell.
A drawing he did at home –
It's a picture of a dinosaur
but he says it's not meant to be me!
He also brought his trumpet;
yes, I know . . .

I expected a loud noise
and got one,
but he's getting the hang of it
and so I made lots of encouraging noises,
not quite as loudly as the trumpet though.

Do you want to take an interest in what the
youngsters do?

Think how you're all family together, working
together for the good of each other.

GOD-CHAT

These commandments that I give you today
are to be on your hearts. Impress them on
your children. Talk about them when you sit
at home and when you walk along the road,
when you lie down and when you get up.

Deuteronomy 6:6, 7 (NIV)

Father God,
thank you for the teaching I received about you.
I did my best to teach my children too
and now it's the turn of my grandchildren
to learn about you.
I want to back up what their parents are
    already doing

but I want to do it in a natural way,
not ramming religion down their throats,
but just chatting,
gossiping the gospel,
as we stroll through the fields,
walk along the road,
or sit and have a snack.
Help me to be sensitive
to my grandchildren,
to listen and observe,
and only talk when it's the right time.

How much do I want my grandchildren to
know about Jesus?

UP-TO-DATE

Jesus Christ is the same yesterday,
today and for ever.

Hebrews 13:8

In a world that's rocking on so fast,
it's a relief, Lord Jesus,
to know that you are, indeed,
the same yesterday,
today,
and for ever.
Sometimes it seems to me
that I can't keep up with
all that's going on,
particularly on the technology front.

Rather than me helping the younger folk,
there's now a major role reversal going on!
They're helping me.
They're completely unfazed by IT
and I'm grateful that they can explain things
    to me
that I find are beyond my comprehension
    and skill.
Thank you for the knowledge
that is being absorbed into these young brains!

How much do I appreciate the help my
grandchildren give me?

10

COMPLIMENT AND COMPLEMENT

**How wonderful it is, how pleasant,
for God's people to live together in harmony!**

Psalm 133:1

Lord,
it is indeed wonderful
when everything in the family
is hunky-dory
and we all get along together in harmony.
Help me to be generous with compliments,
to affirm every member of the family.
Thank you that each of us has a contribution
to make to the whole.

Thank you for our different skills and abilities,
our different personalities
and our different ages.
May I work hard at holding the family together
on the solid foundation of your love.

Think of families where there isn't harmony.

Maybe in your own family there is tension.

How can you help release some of that tension?

11

PRIVILEGE AND RESPONSIBILITY

May the Lord our God be with us,
as he was with our ancestors; may he
never leave us, or abandon us.

1 Kings 8:57

I realise, Lord,
that it's a great privilege
to be part of a family
and to have grandchildren.
Help me to remember that with privilege
comes responsibility.
May I be a good example
to my grandchildren.

I don't want them to be afraid of me,
nor ashamed of me.
Help me to keep walking with you
so that my grandchildren get a glimpse of you
in me.

In what practical ways do you take the
responsibility of grandparenthood seriously?

TEENS AND BEYOND

SECONDARY SCHOOL

The Lord's unfailing love and
mercy still continue,
fresh as the morning, as sure as the sunrise.
The Lord is all I have,
and so I put my hope in him.

Lamentations 3:22-24

Lord,
I feel nervous.
My granddaughter is starting secondary school.
Surely she's not old enough!
It doesn't seem very long
since I held her as a newborn in my arms.

Well, here she is now
ready to launch forth into a bigger world
than she's known so far.
Will she find her way round?
Will the teachers be kind?
Will she make friends?
I don't know the answers
but I thank you for that promise
of your faithfulness.
May she latch onto your promise
to be with her each new day.
Help her, and help her parents
as she starts this latest stage
of life's adventure.

Remember to pray for all adolescents as they
face new and challenging situations.

A GROWING BODY

You created every part of me;
you put me together in my mother's womb ...
You saw me before I was born.
The days allotted to me
had all been recorded in your book
before any of them ever began.

Psalm 139:13, 16

Only our amazing creator God
could have thought up
a human body.
It's so extraordinary, Lord,
so intricate,

so complex,
so unfathomable.
After eleven years or so
from birth to adolescence,
my grandchild has learnt to
smile,
sit up,
walk,
run,
do sums,
read,
learn an instrument,
and all the rest.
Now it's time to grow up even more.
Be with these young people
as their bodies change
and grow towards adulthood.
It's a confusing time
physically,
and emotionally.

Ponder the wonder of the human body.

PEACEMAKER

When we are punished, it seems to us at
the time something to make us sad, not
glad. Later, however, those who have been
disciplined by such punishment reap the
peaceful reward of a righteous life.

Hebrews 12:11

Lord,
teenage years can be a bit traumatic,
to say the least.
Help my children
to be peacemakers
when there are disagreements
in the family.

The squabbles of childhood
may be past history
but I know from our children
that adolescents will challenge
their parents
and maybe even their grandparents!
Help me to be a peacemaker
when I need to be.

Are there practical ways in which you can help
in the family to bring peace and tranquillity -
without interfering?

4

RELATIONSHIPS

**Some friendships do not last, but some friends
are more loyal than brothers.**

Proverbs 18:24

O Lord,
I recall the tiffs
that my daughter had with her friends.
One day they'd be friends,
the next they'd be at loggerheads.
These days, with social media,
such tiffs can get out of hand.
And then there's the time
when relationships become more serious
and you think, 'Is this the one?'

Sometimes it turns out to be,
sometimes it doesn't.
Help me to have a listening ear
if my grandchild wants to share cares
and give me wisdom to support my
   own children
as they face the challenges of these years.

I need to keep open the communication
channels between us all.

WALK AND TALK

'Tell your children and your grandchildren
about the day you stood in the presence
of the Lord your God . . .'

Deuteronomy 4:9, 10

Lord,
I'd like to think that my grandson
and granddaughter
will still want to walk and talk
with me as they did when they were nippers.
I remember it wasn't always easy to talk to
    my parents
when I was an adolescent.
I thought they couldn't possibly understand
what was happening in my life.

They were probably much more aware
than I gave them credit for.
But I would like to have had a kind grandma
or a fun-loving grandpa
that I could walk and talk with.
As my grandchildren grow up, Lord,
help me to respect their growing independence
but to keep the door open so they can chat
whenever they want to,
whether on the phone,
in person,
or via the dreaded social media!

What shared interests do you have with your
grandchild? Sport, music, food?

How can you pick up on, and develop, the
snippets of information or questions that come
from your grandchildren?

LOVE FOR ALL

**See how much the Father has loved us!
His love is so great that we are called
God's children.**

1 John 3:1a

I'm a little wary of saying this, Lord,
but sometimes I think I favour
one grandchild more than another.
Help me to treat each one fairly,
to love each one unconditionally
and to work at building good relationships
with each member of the extended family.
Thank you for your immense love
for all people,

for your compassion and kindness,
your protection and fatherly goodness.
May I be so immersed in your love
that it will spill out to my family –
to each and every one of them.

God loves. He loves me. He loves each member
of my family. So must I.

COMMUNICATION

(The Lord) instructed our ancestors
to teach his laws to their children,
so that the next generation might learn them
and in turn should tell their children.
In this way they also would put
their trust in God . . .

Psalm 78:5-7

Above all else, Lord,
I guess the best thing I can do
for my growing grandchildren
is to pray for them,
to commit them to you,
to place them into your loving arms,
to ask you to protect them

and for them to know your love
above all other loves.
But at the same time, Lord,
I do want to communicate with each of them
effectively,
kindly,
and with sympathy, empathy,
and compassion.
As God's children
we should follow your ways.
These days our grandchildren
grow up with messages that tell them
they can live how they like.
Your moral compass can get lost,
even buried,
beneath the clamour of the world's views.
Help our grandchildren to know you
and to follow your wise ways.

Think of practical ways to communicate with
your grandchild.

What do they like best: emails, texts, phone
calls . . . ?

8

SUPPORT

I remember the sincere faith you have,
the kind of faith that your grandmother
Lois and your mother Eunice also had.
I am sure that you have it also.

2 Timothy 1:5

I thank you, heavenly Father,
for the example of my own parents,
for their love for you and for me.
Thank you for the extended family,
and the opportunity to share support
and our faith in you with each other.
Keep us faithful to each other
and to you as we commit each day
to you.

May I affirm my grandchildren.
May they have a sense of self-worth
and confidence that you have a loving grip
on their lives.

How can I affirm a grandchild who feels useless
or sad?

CHURCH TALK

**Future generations will serve him;
they will speak of the Lord to
the coming generation.**

Psalm 22:30

I'm excited, Lord,
that my grandchild may become
an ambassador for you.
Help me to encourage her
to use her music-making for you,
or her art
or whatever creative juices you've given her.
Thank you for young people
and help us in our churches

to give them opportunities
to serve you.
Help those of us who are older
but not necessarily wiser
to affirm them
as they learn to stand up
in public for you.

Do I need to relinquish some piece of service
for God so that a younger person can do it?

LISTEN

Remember this, my dear brothers and sisters!
Everyone must be quick to listen, but slow
to speak and slow to become angry.

James 1:19

Sometimes I blather on, Lord,
chattering too much
and not listening enough.
Help me to listen to you
and to listen to my grandchildren.
Age difference shouldn't be an obstacle
for listening and sharing.
After all, when we're all part of your family
we're brothers and sisters

whatever the age gap,
so my grandchild is my sibling
in your kingdom!
That's a weird thought . . .
but worth pondering.
Make me take opportunities to be still
in the presence of my grandchildren
and give them the chance to speak.
Help them to know that they're loved.

Am I a chatterbox or a reflective thinker?

When is age difference important in relationships
and when is it irrelevant?

CELEBRATE

Love is patient and kind; it is not jealous
or conceited or proud; love is not
ill-mannered or selfish or irritable; love
does not keep a record of wrongs; love is
not happy with evil, but is happy with
the truth. Love never gives up; and its
faith, hope, and patience never fail.

1 Corinthians 13:4-7

Lord, I want to celebrate
everything about being a grandparent.
It's a joy and a privilege,
a wonderful opportunity to share love.
I rejoice today that I'm a grandparent.

I love my children
and I love my grandchildren.
Thank you for all the opportunities
we have to celebrate family life together.
May we never give up on love and life.

Think how best you like to celebrate – and plan
a party!

FOR YOUR OWN
REFLECTIONS AND PRAYERS

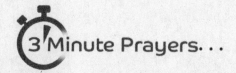

3'Minute Prayers. . .

Before I Sleep
1501601

For the Morning
1501603

For the Weekend
1501604

For Coffee Breaks
1501605

For the Evening
1501607

www.kevinmayhew.com